Unlock Your Full Potential

AF080811

OrangeBooks Publication

Smriti Nagar, Bhilai, Chhattisgarh - 490020

Website: **www.orangebooks.in**

© Copyright, 2022, Author

All rights reserved. No part of this book may be reproduced, stored in a retrieval system, or transmitted, in any form by any means, electronic, mechanical, magnetic, optical, chemical, manual, photocopying, recording or otherwise, without the prior written consent of its writer.

First Edition, 2022

Unlock Your Full Potential

How To Unlock Your Full Potential
So You Can Attract All Your Desires

Mustafa Mun

OrangeBooks Publication
www.orangebooks.in

UNLOCK YOUR FULL POTENTIAL

How To Unlock Your Full Potential So You Can Attract All Your Desires

Disclaimer

This eBook has been written for informational purposes only. Every effort has been made to make this eBook as complete and accurate as possible. However, there may be mistakes in typography or content. Also, this eBook provides information only up to the publishing date. Therefore, this eBook should be used as a guide, not as the ultimate source.

The purpose of this eBook is to educate. The author and publisher make no warranty that the information in this eBook is complete and are not liable for any errors or omissions.The author and publisher will have no liability or responsibility to any person or entity for any loss or damage caused or alleged to be caused by this ebook, whether directly or indirectly.

This eBook offers information and is designed for educational purposes only. You should not rely on this information as a substitute, nor does it replace professional medical advice, diagnosis, or treatment.

Index

Introduction 2

Committing to the Process 5
- You Might Not Always Feel Like It 6
- Just Go With It 7
- Include Other People 7

Define Your Own Potential 9
- Prioritize Your Health 10
- Make Time To Disconnect 10
- Make Time To Do Therapy 11
- Connect To Yourself Through Creativity 12
- Try Meditation 12
- Define Your Goals 13
- Make Conscious Efforts 13
- Set Up Milestones 14

Use The Law Of Attraction To Make Your Desires A Reality 16
- Manifesting With The Law Of Attraction 16

Habits Begin With One Small Step .. 21

Let Go And Prosper 26
- Old Habits 26
- Relationships 27
- Gaining More Wisdom And Understanding 28

Use Metrics To Optimize You 30
- Monitor Daily Progress 31
- Upgrade Your Goals 31
- Plan Everything Ahead 32
- Consider Using An App 32

Pitfalls Are A Part Of The Process 35
- Understand the Pitfalls 35
- Grieve for a Short Time After Pitfalls 36
- Accept the Pitfall As-Is 36
- Learn from the Pitfall 37

Unlocking Your Potential Is Not A Destination 39
- Stop And Think For Awhile 40
- Practice Yoga 40
- Tap Into Your Self Knowledge 41

Conclusion 44

Introduction

Introduction

If you are looking to unlock your full potential, you might be wondering what the first steps you can take to attract all the desires you have into your life. Unlocking your potential might seem complicated if you are unsure of how to start the process. If you have been stuck in a dead-end job or other life ruts, unlocking your full potential now is more important than ever before.

Potential is also different for every unique person. You need to define what potential looks like for you, as it might be different for you than for other people in your life. If your process looks different than the other people around you, try not to put too much thought into it or compare yourself to others. Unlocking your full potential is a personal journey that shouldn't be compared to the others around you.

The e-book will go through all the steps you need to take to attract all your desires. When starting your journey, you first need to figure out what your ideal self is. Without knowing what your ideal self is, you won't be able to define your potential or your desires that need to be fulfilled. Your ideal self is the best version of yourself in every situation.

If you aren't sure how to become the ideal version of yourself, the best rule of thumb to follow is to focus as much as you can. You need to have a clear focus on what you want so that you can focus on each of it and every day. Try to start your day and end your day thinking about this ideal self that you want to become.

Sometimes you also have to do a little bit of pretending. You won't magically become a new person overnight. Think about what you want your reactions to be in every situation, or what you want your life to look like. As soon as you have a clear vision of who you want to be, pretend you are already that person.

Once you have this ideal version of yourself created, you can move on to the official first step of unlocking your potential. In this book, we will outline 7 sections and provide tips for starting the journey to unlock your full potential.

You won't be able to unlock your full potential without following all 7 sections. Following all of them and reviewing them from time to time will help keep you on track and ensure you are going in the right direction. During the steps, make sure you are surrounding yourself with a good company that encourages you and supports you. Having negative people in your life during this time will make it harder to really grasp your full potential and start the process.

If you're ready to get started and you know you're in the right place to unlock your full potential, start reading this full e-book guide today. You won't regret taking these next steps and creating a new you that's ready to take on the world.

Committing to the Process

Committing to the Process

Committing to the process is essential to unlocking your full potential. If you don't commit to the process, nothing will happen. You won't be able to fully start your journey. It's okay to be full of good intentions, but you also need to be able to have a clear idea of how to get where you want to go. Shifting from ideas to actions can be hard. It's easy to daydream about starting something new, but it's a totally different thing to really put those things into action.

Committing to the process means not procrastinating. Procrastination will only lead you to failure and the inability to attract all the desires you want and need. Struggling to see something through is hard for everyone, so don't get discouraged if you are struggling to make your actions real. Just try to stay on track and let go of the things you can't control.

If there are some things in your life that you can't control that are keeping you unmotivated, just try to let them go. Trying to hang onto them will cause the process to last much longer than it needs to. One easy way to commit to the process is to set goals. Without goals, you won't be able to see the progress you are making. If you have clearly defined goals, you can track your progress and know you are doing the best you can. Don't just write down the goals, write down how you will achieve them.

Without clear instructions to follow, you might continue to struggle with not being able to get on track.

Anytime you are committing to the process, you will need to track the how just as much as the why. Knowing all the different processes you can use to get to your destination will help you commit to the process and get to the end result more effectively.

Remember that intentions are only half the commitment. You need to put those intentions into place and start your actions today. Remember that the process requires dedication of time, listening, and intimacy with life. When you commit to the process, you give yourself a better chance of getting to the end result.

You Might Not Always Feel Like It

Remember that you won't always feel like committing to the process. There will be some days where you wake up and feel like you don't want to take any action or move forward. If you always follow your feelings, you will never succeed. You have to keep committing and moving forward, even during the days and weeks where you feel like you're over the process.

It's okay to feel different from day to day, but you need to make sure that you try to move past those feelings and work on your potential every day. Don't be too hard on yourself though. Not completing all the tasks you have laid out for the day is not the end of the world. Just make sure you create more space and more time during the rest of the week to get these things done.

Just Go With It

Just going with it is much easier said than done. If you stumble around pitfalls or there are unexpected things that pop up, just keep the process going. You will need to make the habit of just going with it before it really becomes an easy part of the process. Just going with it needs to become a habit just like brushing your teeth or going to work in the morning. Once you put in the effort to keep going with it, you will unlock more and more of your potential every day.

Include Other People

Some people find it necessary to include others in their process. If you don't have a good support system or people that you trust to be a part of your process, then you might find it better to keep this to yourself. However, if you have someone in your life that could help you, you should definitely include them in this process. You might find that they have good advice for you that you wouldn't have been able to discover by yourself.

Make sure you listen to positive opinions and surround yourself with those who have light in them. Telling other people about your process and goals will ensure you have some accountability. If you are doing someone on your own, it's easy to simply give it up. No one will know you even started, so it will be easy to simply change your plan or track.

If you tell other people though, you will be held accountable. If you are struggling or need help, they can also encourage you on the days you feel down.

Define Your Own Potential

Define Your Own Potential

Before you maximize your potential, you need to define it. If you don't define it, you won't be able to get the most out of it. If you don't know your true purpose, you won't be able to find the potential you need to make the most out of every situation.

Keep in mind that potential is the capacity to transform your life into your highest aspirations and unique goals. This means self-reflecting on your strengths and weaknesses. You need to know what you're good at and then be willing to improve on the things you need to improve on. Before going where you want to go, you need to make sure you know who you are. This will help you make a better plan of action.

Balance is also key to making sure you can uncover your full potential. This means your mind, your body, and your spirit must be in alignment with each other all the time. If one of these components is functioning at a low level, you might find that you don't have a harmonious relationship with yourself. You need to make sure all these things are in line because they are interconnected with each other. Addressing each of the components individually and then together will ensure you can make optimal progress in uncovering your true potential.

Here are some more steps you can take to help you uncover your true potential:

Prioritize Your Health

If you want to uncover your full potential, you need to be honest with yourself and make your mind and body healthy. If you are currently using drugs or alcohol, you might want to consider cutting back until you have your full potential in line and discovered. Decreasing your substance use can also impact your general wellbeing, relationships, and employment for the best.

If you don't have a normal sleep schedule, consider regulating it the best you can. If you sleep and wake up at the same time every day, you are more likely to have more energy and therefore be able to devote more of your time to discovering your true potential and acting out habits that will allow you to do this.

Exercising, eating healthy, and staying hydrated are also important steps to ensure you are making the most out of your health and using it to uncover your potential.

Make Time To Disconnect

If you are constantly surrounded by other people, work duties, and other things that you might think are overwhelming, you need to make sure you are making time to disconnect. This also means taking time away from your phones and computers. Constantly being bombarded by messages and notifications can take time away from your working to uncover your potential.

The main thing to remember is that you want to reconnect with your body. This usually means spending time doing things with your body, such as exercising, painting, or doing something else that will focus your mind and body together at the same time.

You can either turn off your phone for several hours a day or you can put it on silent so that you don't feel the need to look at it as soon as a notification comes through. This will help you reconnect with your heart and your body.

Make Time To Do Therapy

You might think therapy is not for you, or maybe you have had a bad experience with therapy in the past. Trying to be strong when you can't do everything on your own is counterproductive.

You need to be willing to admit you need help and always be willing to give other people a portion of the work instead of overdoing yourself.

If you really want to uncover your full potential and make sure you have people by your side, you might want to consider getting your heart and mind back on track. Only when you are in sync with yourself can you begin to commit to discovering your potential.

Many people also find that they get to know themselves better during therapy. Talking to a therapist might show you your strengths and weaknesses and help you better understand where your potential is coming from.

It will also help you find balance in your day-to-day life. Remember that going to therapy isn't a sign of weakness, it's a sign of strength that you're willing to ask for help.

Connect To Yourself Through Creativity

If you aren't making time for the things you love, you won't be able to realize your potential. Your creativity can come from anything, including poems, painting, or art. If you're not artistic, there are still many other ways you can connect to your creativity. Creativity can mean sports, film making, reading, or making anything that shows you your potential.

When you do the things you love and make a creative effort, you show yourself that your dreams and passions matter. It also allows you to express yourself better. If you're comfortable, you can also share your creativity with other people. This will show others what you're doing to unlock your potential and they can encourage you and help you unlock even more potential.

Try Meditation

The point of meditating is to focus on your breath and let the world fade away from you. Relaxing your mind and body can help you become more in charge of your health and potential.

Meditation will also allow you to stay within the present moment. Tuning yourself into the environment around you will allow you to unlock more and more of the potential around you.

Being secure in your own presence will allow you to connect to the inner power you have in your own body and mind. This will allow you to be more confident and teach you to focus on what's most important.

Meditation will also allow you to be more harmonious and find balance within yourself. This allows you to stay grounded in your potential and be aware of the imbalance you might have in your life. Working on these imbalances during mediation will give your mind time to uncover the true gifts you have to help you unlock the potential within you.

Define Your Goals

Defining goals is a part of uncovering your potential process. This starts by identifying your inner voice. What does your inner voice tell you to be or do? Maybe it's suggesting you change career paths or try new hobbies. If you are stuck in a dead-end job or don't have any hobbies where you can express yourself, these could stifle you from unlocking your potential.

Defining your goals can ensure you are on the right track to manifesting your desires. Try not to make the goals about money or moving up in society. Instead, choose goals that make you want to be a better person.

Make Conscious Efforts

You must make conscious efforts once you have set your goals and are ready to begin bringing your potential into the world.This includes doing many of the steps listed above, such as making a vision board, staying healthy, and considering starting therapy.

Unlocking your personal potential will not come overnight and it won't just begin without any work. You need to work hard to unlock your true potential. You have to work to find the answers. Experimenting with your life and your career choices can be done in this phase. Remember that small steps are sometimes the best steps. If you aren't sure about the decisions you're making, you might want to consider not taking too many steps. Slow and steady movements will ensure you reach your final destination with ease.

Set Up Milestones

Along with defining goals, you should have milestones. This will help you track your progress. If you only have the end goal, you might get discouraged when it's taking you longer than expected to reach it. Having milestones will show you that you are, in fact, making progress even though you haven't reached the finish line yet. Reaching your goal step by step is key.

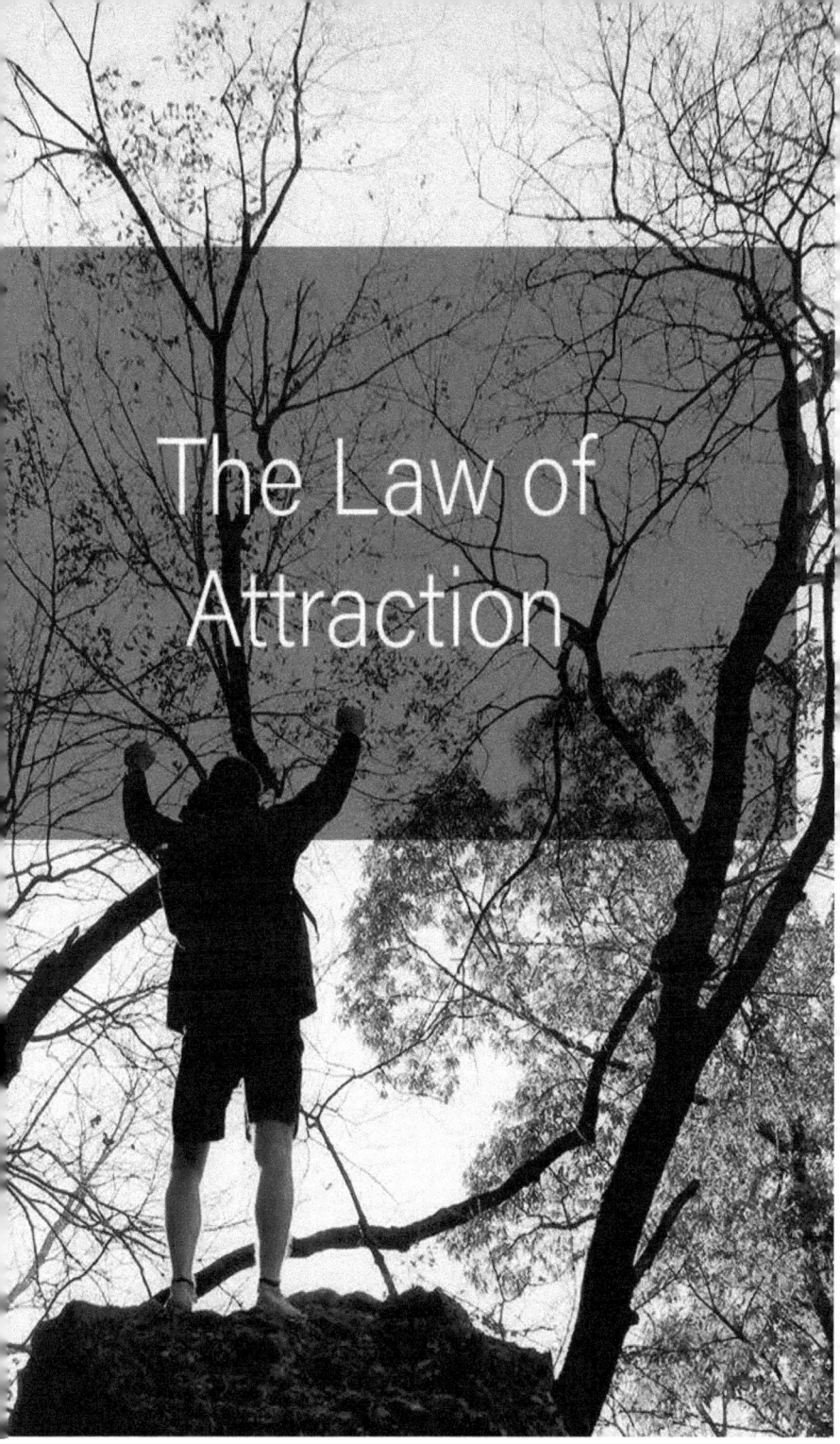

Use The Law Of Attraction To Make Your Desires A Reality

The Law of Attraction is gaining traction in various communities because of all the people that have found confidence and practicality in its principles. It simply states that like attracts like. This means that if you are putting good vibes and confidence into the atmosphere, your environment will give it back to you.

By putting forth good energy, you will also receive good energy back. The same goes for if you begin to think negatively. Thinking negatively will only bring about negative thoughts. If you are constantly putting yourself and others down, you will feel the same negative energy from others.

Manifesting With The Law Of Attraction

Manifesting is a common part of the Law of Attraction. You can manifest your desires by putting them forth into the world and imagining yourself having them. Manifesting comes with many techniques that you need to memorize and try so that you can try to manifest your desires much more quickly. Remember that manifesting is an attraction technique that you will need to take the time to make a habit out of.

The first and easiest way to manifest your desires is to use sensory visualization. You will need to have a vivid imagination for this to work, so make sure to use all your senses. Imagine yourself the way you want to be, using all of your 5 senses. Having all your senses on board will ensure you get a clear picture of all the things you desire.

Vision boards are also another fantastic way to envision your future and the way you want your potential to look and be. Vision boards are also part of dream boarding. You can print off pictures from the internet or you can draw and paint pictures yourself. You can also use inspirational quotes as well as pictures. This will ensure you get a good mix of visual cues and reading cues. Make sure you put the vision board in a place you will see it often and every day. Seeing it right when you wake up will also ensure you start your day on the right track.

Many phycologists have evidence that vision boards work. They say it helps you eliminate problems that might be in the way of you envisioning your dreams. Looking at the vision board every day will also ensure you are being reminded of your goals and you are easily manifesting them into reality.

Eliminating self-limiting beliefs is also important. You need to rely on your own self-perseverance. Your self-perseverance is all that matters when it comes to conquering your habits and realizing your full potential.

You should try to do conscious belief assessments. Is there anything you think about yourself and the life that you've created that could be negatively impacting you? Make sure to get rid of those thoughts immediately.

Don't let any thoughts undermine your ability to form your new full potential. You also need to be supportive of your thoughts. This means always thinking clean thoughts about yourself and not letting negative energy into your space and mind.

Gratitude journaling is also another main way that people manifest their desires. Part of manifesting new things is to make sure you are thankful for everything you already have. Gratitude journaling can ensure you remember all the things that are most important to you.

You can choose to write in the journal every day or you can spend a few hours a week writing down everything you are thankful for. This will put good vibrational energy into the world, and will make it more likely that you will receive good energy back.

Multi-perspective visualization is when you get an outsider's point of view. This goes back to sharing your dreams and thoughts with other people. Having another vantage point will ensure you get where you want to go faster. People that are on the outside of the situation will be able to offer up views and help that you might not be able to see on your own.

Having another set of eyes will help you make more informed and detached observations. This will allow you to better problem solve the issues at hand. Don't ever forget to use your own perspective as well though. Both perspectives are important. Your own perspective will invoke more emotion which is also important when it comes to unlocking your full potential.

Another important tip to follow is manifestation affirmations. Affirmations are meant to be positive statements used to help eradicate negative tendencies that you might be prone to. You always need to reinforce your own empowerment and make sure you have all the things you need to achieve your dreams.

This means you need to think constant positive thoughts about yourself, including "I'm worthy of receiving the things I desire" and "I will continue to work wholeheartedly towards the goals that I want to manifest."

Focus wheels are also important. Making a focus wheel is extremely easy which makes it one of the top tools used for manifesting. You can simply draw a small circle on the paper and write down all the goals and dreams you wish to achieve. You can also do it on a whiteboard if you prefer for it to be a larger size.

The last thing you can do is to begin to act like you already have the desire. Acting like you already have it in your grasp will ensure you manifest it quicker. Following all of these manifesting techniques will ensure you get everything you want.

Habits Begin With One Small Step

Habits Begin With One Small Step

Every journey and every step starts with one step. People often think that change has to be huge and monumental. Some people also think that habits and change need to start with a large and life-changing step. While this could be true, it usually doesn't work like that for everyone. Don't be ashamed of the small steps and don't think they aren't as important. Start with small steps and work towards the bigger ones. Many small steps can also equal larger steps.

Your life can change permanently with small steps just as they can with large steps. Remember that small steps are also easier to make habits with. For example, if you want to start eating healthy, you should take the steps slowly. Incorporate more fruits and vegetables while still eating some of the foods you normally eat. If you throw away all the diet stables you're used to and try to only eat healthily, you might find that this diet and habit aren't sustainable.

The same goes for reading, journaling, or making new life routines. You might still find some comfort in your old routines and habits and that's okay. You can still incorporate new habits into your old routine instead of overhauling everything you're used to.

Just make sure you have strategies for moving forward and that you are consistently moving forward with these strategies.

Make sure to always reward yourself when it comes to making and forming new habits. Rewarding yourself might seem silly at the beginning, but you are your biggest supporter during this time of change.

The rewards can be small or large, but always make sure you are giving yourself space and time to accept the rewards. Giving yourself rewards will also ensure you make an immediate practice of the habit because you will look forward to the rewards.

Try to make new habits easy instead of overwhelming yourself with huge changes. For example, if you want to spend more time exercising, you might want to consider spending time exercising at home for only 20 minutes a day before hitting up the gym for hours at a time.

If you go too far in too quickly, you will find yourself overworked and not ready to take on the challenge. Don't underestimate how much a small habit can make a difference.

The best way to form new habits is to think about the habits you need to uncover your potential. What habits do you need to start your new career? What habits do you need to form to get you where you need to go?

Experts have come up with four questions to ask yourself when forming new habits. These questions can help you learn to form new habits with small steps:

- **How can I make it easy?** How can you make your new habit easy to follow? If you make it too hard or out of reach, you will see that the habit will quickly drop out of your mind, and you won't feel encouraged to keep it.

- **How can I make it attractive?** How can you make the habit attractive to follow? If you enjoy doing it, you will be more likely to follow it. Of course, not all new habits can be exciting. Try to make new habits attractive in at least one area though.

- **How can I make it obvious?** The habit needs to be obvious and memorable so that you follow it. For example, if you want to start taking supplements every day, put them in an easy-to-see spot near water where you will remember to take them as you're drinking.

- **How can I make it satisfying?** Think of ways you can make the new habit satisfying and rewarding. This will encourage you to follow it and make it even more of a practice than before.

These four rules will not make every new habit immediately, but they will help you to stay on track to achieve your goals faster. It will also help you do what you say you're going to do. By moving step by step, you will keep yourself encouraged and ready to take on every new day.

Once you have the new habit, you can start to increase it in small ways. Start small and build on that small as well. As you build the habits, try breaking them into small sections to make them easier to remember. Keeping the habits, a reasonable size will ensure you are building the right amount of momentum. For example, if you want to work out for 40 minutes a day but don't think you'll feel up to it, you can work out twice in 20-minute sections. You can also break the exercises up into reps so that they go by quicker and easier.

Don't be hard on yourself if you slip up. If you lose control, you are fully capable of putting yourself back on track. Just make sure you get yourself back on your feet as soon as possible. The longer you wait, the harder it will be to get back on track.

Remember that making a plan for failure doesn't mean you are anticipating and expecting failure. It just means that you are prepared for it and there is nothing wrong with ensuring you are prepared and ready.

Make a list of situations or emergencies that could potentially pull you off track. Knowing the situations that could distract you will help you better prepare for the future. Remember that it's more important to be patient and consistent than perfect. Don't strive for perfectionism because you will never get there. Just stay consistent in your habits.

Make sure you are sticking to your pace and plan. As long as you are sticking to a pace for making new habits that you can handle, you shouldn't have any problem staying on track with your habits, the small ones and the big ones.

Let Go And Prosper

If you want to prosper and move forward to unlock your potential, you need to let go of the past. Harboring bad feelings from the past will only keep you trapped in bad habits and even worse thoughts. In order to move forward and manifest your desires, you need to let go of everything in your past that has negatively impacted you.

This could be past relationships, past jobs, or past trauma. Sit down and think about what things you are holding onto from the past that keep you from moving forward. They might be hard to confront, but you need to face them head-on so you can let go.

If there is anyone you need to talk to you help you let go, consider having those hard situations to make it better for your future and the future of the other person. You will be surprised how much better you feel and how much quicker you prosper with your goals and potential.

This also means you need to let go of all the toxic things going on in your life. Some common things that can be toxic that you need to let go of so you can prosper include:

Old Habits

Many old habits might be holding you back, some of which might not even be in the front of your brain. Some examples of old habits that could be holding you back might include smoking, reality television, sleeping too much, or eating something that's not good for you.

You might not know how much something is holding you back until you get past it and move on. You can begin to try new things and see how the new habits have a positive impact on your life. You will soon notice yourself getting rid of the toxic things in your life and you will be finding new things that you love.

Relationships

I think everyone knows how toxic relationships can be. It can be hard, breaking it off with someone who might be toxic though because there might have been a time when you really loved them and you could have some very good memories with them. Deciding that a relationship is toxic and moving on is one of the toughest things in life. However, it must be done if you want to uncover your full potential.

Allow yourself some of the hard conversations even though it could be difficult to get the words out. Make sure you have closure with the other person, or you might not be able to fully move on. Simply blocking them or refusing to respond to them might be the trick. If the relationship is abusive or they gaslight you, it could be a better idea not to sit down and talk to them. However, blocking them and refusing to contact them doesn't work for everyone.

Some people cannot truly move on unless they sit with the other person and have a deep conversation about how they need to move on. If the relationship is abusive, consider bringing someone with you to talk to the other person who can make you feel safer.

Gaining More Wisdom And Understanding

If you want to let go, you will need to remove yourself from the negative and life-draining people in your life. Think of all the people in your life and try to think of the ones that make positive contributions and the ones that are affecting you negatively.

You can also choose to spend more time with people who, like you, are trying to discover their potential and gain wisdom. This will encourage you to stay on track and it will also help you receive the advice you might need.

Overall, remember that trying to hold onto habits and bad relationships can cause you unnecessary suffering. While you're suffering, you won't be able to unlock your true potential.

You will be stuck in one place until you acknowledge the things that are holding you back.

Use Metrics To Optimize You

Use Metrics To Optimize You

Even though you might not be a fan of measuring and tracking yourself with numbers, metrics are a part of optimizing yourself. Measuring progress can take the form of many different things and ways. If you're good with computers, you can track your progress with spreadsheets or other software that you might be good at using.

If you don't love measurements or using computer tools, you can simply track your progress with a notebook or journal. You also want to make sure you aren't aimlessly working too hard without making any real progress. Just because you are working hard doesn't mean you are making the optimal amount of progress. Measuring can show you ways that you can cut back on work and make more progress. Don't get the process wrong though, you always have to work hard when it comes to unlocking your potential.

Measuring can ensure you are making the maximum amount of progress possible though.

The easiest way to do this is to make thorough checklists and task management systems. This allows you to mark off and check things as you complete them. You also need to think about the quality of the tasks. For example, if you see that you are accomplishing many tasks in one day, but you aren't seeing too much progress, you might need to rethink the quality of those tasks. Maybe you're accomplishing a lot of tasks but those tasks are not really doing a lot when it comes to your end game plan.

Monitor Daily Progress

You also need to monitor your progress daily. Weekly and monthly progress tracking are not enough. Goal tracking can be done weekly though. You can take a weekly goal and break it up into daily tasks. This allows for weekly and daily progress tracking.

Breaking down the task into smaller tasks will give you the feeling that you are getting more done. If you have a large task or a large goal, you might find yourself waiting weeks or months to get it done. This can easily be discouraging, especially if you have a personality type that likes to see things being deleted or checked off a list.

Breaking goals into small tasks gives you the power to check off or cross off items on your to-do list every single day. If nothing else, this makes you feel accomplished and gives you the push and drive to keep going.

Upgrade Your Goals

As you move along the journey of unlocking your full potential, you might find that you set some goals too low. This is a great discovery, and you can begin to change your goals as you see this happening. As you keep making personal progress, you can update and upgrade your goals. With progress, you will find that some of your goals become too easy. While it's great to accomplish easy goals, ensure that you are also continuously challenging yourself.

Upgrading the goal doesn't always mean changing it completely. If you are doing a weight loss journey as part of uncovering your potential, you might find that you are getting through the planned workouts and diet plan much easier than anticipated. This means you can add more workouts or maybe change the ones you have currently to make them harder.

As you can see, you're not changing the overall goal, you're just making it more in line with your current accomplishments.

Realizing you can upgrade your goals is a great feeling and will give you an extra push to possibly uncover your potential sooner than you expected.

Plan Everything Ahead

You have to plan ahead for any real accomplishment. You won't get to where you want to go without a plan. Without a plan, you might even find yourself wandering around aimlessly, not sure how to get to the next step. With a concrete plan laid out before you get started, you'll be more likely to find yourself making progress.

Consider Using An App

Even if you aren't tech-savvy, there are many optimization apps and progress tracking apps that are easy to use. Having it right on your phone will also encourage you to actually use it because of its convenience. If you prefer the paper and pen approach, do whatever makes you feel comfortable. However, many people find that apps encourage them to dedicate more time to metrics and goal tracking.

Some apps can also show your entire project, your habits, your averages, and your target. The app or method you use doesn't have to be expensive or complicated, it just has to work for you and the process you are following to unlock your potential.

Remember that no matter what kind of metrics you choose to optimize yourself, don't spend too much time planning. Some people never actually get to their real goals and progress because they spend too much time planning.

Spending too much time planning might mean you are scared to actually start the process. Try to get past this step. You also don't have to plan from start to finish, you just need to have the beginning to get you started.

Pitfalls Are A Part Of The Process

Pitfalls Are A Part Of The Process

When you start a new life-changing journey, there are bound to be some pitfalls. These are part of the process of changing and growing. No process or change can be accomplished without pitfalls. Preparing for them from the beginning can ensure you don't get stuck when they happen.

If you are expecting them, you can make a game plan. Mistakes and pitfalls are a part of life and can't be avoided. Remember that pitfalls can either burden you or motivate you to move forward.

Remember that you can not undo or redo past mistakes. You just need to learn to live with them and move on. Of course, this is always easier said than done.

Understand the Pitfalls

Regret when you encounter a pitfall can cause you to feel bad and constantly have thoughts about everything you can do better. This is not a good way to live. You can regret things you did do and things you didn't do.

Try to identify where the pitfall is and from where the regrets are coming. This will allow you to move on easily. You also need to understand your rationale behind the decision you made or didn't make. Knowing why you did something will allow you to not make the same mistakes in the future.

Grieve for a Short Time After Pitfalls

Before immediately moving on from a pitfall, take a short time to grieve. Before you can accept the mistake or the wrong that happened, you need to grieve the regrets and prepare for the change that is coming your way.

If you encounter a pitfall that seems like you can't overcome or move past, consider reaching out to friends or family for support. If the pitfall was your wrongdoing, you can also apologize to the person you might have wronged. If the pitfall isn't your fault, try to forgive the other person and begin to take steps to move forward.

Make sure you demonstrate to the other person that he or she hurt you and explain to them that you can't have them around your process if they will continue to cause pitfalls. Make sure you are always expressing your negative emotions so that you can move past them sooner. If you don't express your feelings, you will just end up holding them in and it will be harder for you to move on.

Accept the Pitfall As-Is

Don't try to change the pitfall or make a difference after it has happened. This never works. If you don't accept the pitfall as it is, then you won't be able to move on in a timely manner. You will be stuck in the same spot until you accept the pitfall, which can take a long time if you don't do it from the very beginning.

You have no choice but to accept what has happened. This is easier said than done, but you still want to make sure you try your best. You won't always be able to completely let go of the consequences, but you can stop obsessing over them.

Learn from the Pitfall

Once you have experienced a pitfall, you need to learn from the mistakes that got you there so you can move on. Avoid the behaviour or decision that brought you to the mistake in the first place. There is also a lesson to learn when it comes to pitfalls and unwanted consequences.

Sit down with your journal or vision board that you made as part of the process earlier and think about how the pitfall could be avoided. Make detailed notes and make sure you have a plan in place to make sure it never happens again.

Be deliberate and active when it comes to learning from the pitfalls. If you sit idle for too long, you will find yourself backtracking and not able to move on.

Pitfalls are necessary. If you didn't have any pitfalls, you wouldn't be able to truly uncover your potential. Pitfalls will help you identify your strengths and weaknesses, which is a huge part of uncovering your potential.

Do what you can to let go of the past. If you are having trouble, consider bringing it up at your next therapy session or ask a friend for advice. There is no shame in making mistakes and needing help to get past them.

Once you come to realize that everyone will experience pitfalls, you can seek encouragement and help to help you move along in the process.

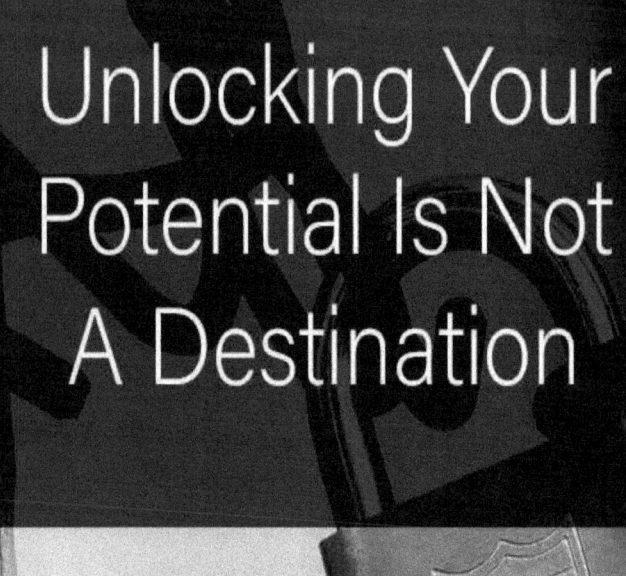
Unlocking Your Potential Is Not A Destination

Unlocking Your Potential Is Not A Destination

The last thing to keep in mind on this journey to unlocking your potential is to remember that it's not a destination. You won't wake up one day and magically have all your potential at your fingertips. Truly unlocking your full potential means you need to sit down and examine your life and your choices. Only then can you truly unlock your potential.

Remember that you will constantly be unlocking your potential because it's not a destination. It might seem strange to constantly be working on something or constantly be working on yourself, but that's how potential works.

Remember that you are dreaming big, but you are starting small. Starting small means you will have a long process ahead of you. While unlocking your potential might not fully be a destination, you will still see goals being mastered and progress being made.

Since the potential is not a destination, it's even more imperative that you try to keep track of goals and make sure your steps of progress are constantly evolving. Without doing this, you will never truly know if you are unlocking your potential or not, because there is no true end goal or end product.

The steps outlined below will help you as you go through the journey, not the destination.

Stop And Think For Awhile

Before starting on the journey of untapping into that potential that's locked away, try to stop and rest for a while. Your life is probably so busy. This is one of the reasons you might feel trapped and unable to uncover your potential. The business of life can make you feel small and not give you enough space to truly grow and create your potential.

Part of stopping to rest also means being mindful of what's going on around you. While unlocking your potential should never be a comparison, you can still take time to note what others are doing around you.

You can also be mindful of what others are doing and try to seek some advice or tips from them to help your journey along. You also need to be mindful of yourself and pay attention to what you're doing individually. When you're driving, just drive and listen to music. Don't get distracted by thoughts, the phone, or other outside factors that are going on around you.

Practice Yoga

Practicing yoga or another mindfulness exercise will ensure you are in the moment and not thinking about the destination. Many people who practice yoga say they feel more mindful and they are more concerned about what's happening to them right now rather than focusing so far into the future.

Thinking about the future is never a bad idea, but it shouldn't come with feelings of anxiety or nervousness. Instead, try to focus on the here and now, even when you aren't doing yoga.

Tap Into Your Self Knowledge

Part of realizing that potential is not a destination is trying to tap into your self-knowledge. Getting to know yourself better and in a more enlightened way will ensure you are trying your best to discover your potential. Focusing on being self-aware will also take your thoughts away from constantly trying to reach the destination.

Once you learn your own self-knowledge, you will also find yourself focusing more and more on getting to know yourself. If you are spending time thinking about things other than just trying to finish the project, you will distract yourself.

Realizing that potential doesn't have a destination can be a hard task for some. For many people, they want there to be an end game and they want to see the end results. Trying to get over this mentality can be hard for most people.

However, learning to be in the moment and just take the journey is an important life discovery. By taking small steps at a time, you can be sure you are moving forward, even when you might not be completely done. Remember that your potential is never finished, so why should there be a final destination?

Uncovering your potential is a life process that's exciting and worthwhile. Your potential is endless and so is your creativity and the things you can make better in this world.

Conclusion

Conclusion

Uncovering your potential is a process and a journey. Hopefully, this e-book has given you some guidance and shown you how tapping into your potential can be just around the corner.

Remember that you will have to break some bad habits and maybe get out of some toxic relationships before you can really start focusing on your potential. Getting rid of the bad and moving on to the good is a crucial step in getting to know your true potential.

You also need to commit to the process you are starting. Without that commitment, you will find yourself lagging and unable to accomplish your true goals. With some commitment and goal setting, you will be well on your way to tapping into the potential you have had locked away for the last several years. During this step, you also need to believe in yourself and remember that you are one of your biggest advocates during this journey.

If you feel overwhelmed, make sure to seek advice and encouragement from those you trust. If you don't have anyone in your personal life with whom you are willing to share, you might want to consider seeing a therapist or counselor.

Professional people can help you get on the right track by offering you wisdom and advice that you might not be able to find on your own. Remember that seeking help from others shows you are brave and willing to seek help. It's not a sign of weakness.

Using metrics or some kind of measurement tool is key to tracking your progress. Knowing your goals are being accomplished will encourage you to keep going, despite any drawbacks. Make sure you use an organized method to keep track of all your goals and successes.

Another important thing to remember is that pitfalls are part of the process. Preparing yourself for them and learning how to overcome them will allow you to move forward without spending too much time regretting and grieving. All journeys and processes have pitfalls. Pitfalls don't mean failure.

The last and most important takeaway from this e-book is to remember that unlocking your potential is not a destination, it will be a lifelong journey from the day you start. While this might be distressing or confusing to some, remember that this just means you always have more potential waiting to be uncovered.

This should encourage you. If you are stuck in a rut or aren't sure what to do next, remember you are still on the journey and you always have more progress to make. Uncovering your true and full potential is exciting and will change the way you live your life forever.

www.ingramcontent.com/pod-product-compliance
Lightning Source LLC
LaVergne TN
LVHW061603070526
838199LV00077B/7161